Trouble Ahead.

My piano lesson was almost over when Jason arrived carrying a big bunch of roses. He had on cowboy boots and a cowboy hat and Miss Jones looked at him as if he were Robert Redford. "Am I too early? I couldn't think of anything else to do outside."

"No, it's okay." She took the roses from him. "They're gorgeous." She stood on her toes and kissed him. Then she turned to me. "You're staying for our party, aren't you, Annie?"

"If you still want me to."

"Of course we want you to. It's not going to be much of a party. . ."

"That's all right," I said.

I should have gone home. I should have said I had to meet my mother; I should have known how angry I was, and how angry I was going to be. . . .

Books by Hila Colman

Accident
Claudia, Where Are You?
Confession of a Storyteller
Diary of a Frantic Kid Sister
Don't Tell Me That You Love Me
Nobody Has to Be a Kid Forever
Tell Me No Lies
What's the Matter with the Dobsons?

Available from ARCHWAY paperbacks

Confession Of A Storyteller

Hila Colman

AN ARCHWAY PAPERBACK
Published by POCKET BOOKS • NEW YORK

Cover photo: Steinway piano courtesy of Steinway and Sons,
New York, New York

 An Archway Paperback published by
POCKET BOOKS, a division of Simon & Schuster, Inc.
1230 Avenue of the Americas, New York, N.Y. 10020

Published by arrangement with Crown Publishers, Inc.
Library of Congress Catalog Card Number: 81-17325

ISBN: 0-671-45659-8

First Pocket Books printing April, 1984

10 9 8 7 6 5 4 3 2 1

AN ARCHWAY PAPERBACK and colophon are
trademarks of Simon & Schuster, Inc.

Printed in the U.S.A.

IL 6+

For Shirley and Kathleen, for good reasons

Confession
Of A Storyteller

1

In *spite* *of* *everything* *that* *hap-*
pened I will always think of Miss Jones as a
very special person. Certainly I never meant to
hurt her. I guess you could say that I idealized
her and thought she was different from ordinary people. I still think that when I first met
her, she was. She was a spiritual person, a
person who looked for beauty in life. Her
music and nature—walking in the woods,
growing flowers—were what was important to
her. As she often said to me, she didn't give a
fig for material possessions, for clothes and
cars and such things. "If I can play my music
and dig in my garden," she used to say, "I am

perfectly happy." That, of course, was before Jason appeared on the scene.

I guess I should start at the beginning which, incredible as it seems, was just a year ago when I was twelve. I wouldn't have thought there could be so much difference between twelve and thirteen: that at twelve you could be so out of it, know so little, and feel that everyone was leaving you behind; then, a short year later, you feel as though you've grown ten years instead of only one.

To be perfectly honest, and I intend to tell the absolute truth here, I think my trouble started with Caroline's party before school opened. My mom thinks that Annie's aberration, as she calls it, began at school when I first met Miss Jones. But Mom doesn't know all the complications between Caroline and me. She still thinks I had a good time at Caroline's party. I never have told her what actually happened that night.

Caroline was my best friend—I might say my only real friend, at least I thought she was. We live in Half-Mile Brook, Connecticut, and if you don't have a car you're stuck. You can't go anywhere, except certain places on a bike, and I wasn't allowed to ride on the highway—the only road out of the dead-end circle where our house is. My mom worked, and when I came home from school on the bus, that was it. I was glad Caroline, who was nine months older than I, lived a few houses away. Although we sometimes had our differences, we were glad to have each other.

Caroline's birthday was at the end of August and she decided to have a party Labor Day weekend. She was making a big thing out of being thirteen (she had started calling herself a teenager at the beginning of the summer) and she thought it was fantastic that there would be thirteen at her party. Six boys and seven girls including herself. Being the youngest I should have suspected that I would end up being the thirteenth.

The day before the party I was at Caroline's house almost all day helping to get things ready. I was making brownies and Caroline was decorating cookies. "I can't wait for tomorrow night," she said. "I've got a new dress."

"I know, you told me." She had, several times. "It's your birthday, you should have one. I guess I'll wear my lavender skirt and the blouse that matches. I don't know why I say I guess, it's all I've got."

Caroline stood back to admire her cookies.

3

She was very pretty. She had a perm for her birthday and her hair was in little curls all over her head. She had much more of a figure than I had, and now, with her flushed face and her summer tan, she looked beautiful. I remember thinking I was glad she was my best friend, which I suppose made what happened later even worse.

"I think my folks are going to be out for part of the evening tomorrow," Caroline said. Her blue eyes sparkled and there was a funny smile on her face. I was not as sophisticated as Caroline—she had even gone to Ireland with her parents and corresponded with a boy she met in Dublin—but I knew what she meant— that is, in a hazy way, not from personal experience. It meant that when her parents were gone, Caroline would turn out all the lights and everyone would disappear, and I would be left alone because I didn't have a boyfriend. The sweet smell of the brownies suddenly made me feel sick.

Until this past summer it hadn't made much difference that Caroline was older and that most of the kids I went around with in school were too. But then Caroline decided she only wanted to go to the lake when the boys were there, and she always wanted to go downtown when she knew the boys had finished playing soccer and would be there too. She hardly ever wanted to go for a hike in the woods with me or play a game at my house, but all summer I still considered her my best friend.

My mom knew the minute I came home from Caroline's that I was feeling gloomy. "What's the matter?" she asked.

"I don't know if I want to go to Caroline's party," I said.

"Why not? You've been talking about it all week. What happened?"

"Nothing happened. I just don't feel like it, that's all."

Mom looked at me with that "I wonder if you're sick" look, but I wasn't, and she knew it. "Something must have happened."

"All those kids are older than I am," I mumbled.

"Oh, for heaven's sake. They're just a few months older. Maybe a year. That's silly, Annie." She laughed. "That's what you get for being smart."

"I wish I weren't." We'd only lived in Half-Mile Brook a couple of years and the first day of school they hadn't known what to do with me. I'd already had a lot of the stuff they were taking in my grade, but since the school was departmentalized, they could put me in a lot of classes a year ahead of my homeroom. That's how I was always the youngest.

I couldn't explain to Mom that there were big differences between twelve and thirteen; she wouldn't have understood. I guess when you get older it doesn't matter. My mom is four years younger than Dad, but they seem just the same. With kids it's different; the older ones make such a big thing of being older.

As usual when I'm down in the dumps, I went out to the garden. I love to put my hands into the earth, to plant things and to watch them grow. I do most of the gardening in our family. My dad gets the soil ready in the spring and Mom helps with the planting. I take care of the plants. We have a fairly large vegetable garden that keeps me busy. You have to pick things when they're ready; otherwise they rot or the animals get them. We have flowers too, but I like growing vegetables better. It's nice to eat carrots or lettuce or a melon you've planted, watched grow, and picked fresh from your own backyard.

I did a little weeding and tied up some tomato plants that were falling over, but I kept thinking about Caroline and her party. Then I thought about Brian Shelton. He just popped into my head out of the blue. He was kind of nice-looking, but not handsome the way Caroline's friend Ken was. Brian wore glasses and wasn't very tall, but when he smiled he looked as if he meant it. Brian was thirteen and a half, close to fourteen, I think, and he never looked at me, except once that summer when we went for a bike ride together. We hardly talked. We just rode our bikes, but I pretended he was my boyfriend and that he had given me the little gold heart I wore on a chain around my neck. My Aunt Molly had given it to me for my birthday but I didn't think she'd mind if I pretended for a little while that it had been a gift from Brian.

Brian's house is behind ours, and he came out into his yard just then. It made me feel funny thinking about him and then having him suddenly appear. "Hi, Annie," he said.

"Hi."

"You going to Caroline's party?"

"Sure. Aren't you?"

"I guess so," he said.

He didn't sound enthusiastic. "Don't you want to go?"

"I don't know. I don't like parties much."

"Neither do I."

Brian was surprised. "I thought all girls liked

7

parties. When my sister goes to a party you'd think she was going to a ball."

I wished I could think of something bright and witty to say back but I couldn't. I certainly wasn't going to tell him that I thought his sister looked silly wearing high heels with her jeans and heavy mascara when she went swimming.

"See you later," Brian said, and he picked up his bike from the driveway and rode off. I kept thinking about him. We could have had a different conversation: "I don't like parties, unless someone I like's going to be there," Brian might have said. "You will go, won't you?"

"I guess so." I wouldn't have sounded too anxious.

"I'm glad. Then I'll surely be there." Before he left he would have given me a long, lingering look until I turned away, my cheeks crimson.

When I went back into the house Mom was upstairs in her bedroom. I asked her if I could wear her amethyst earrings to Caroline's party. "They match my lavender blouse," I said.

Mom smiled. "I thought you weren't interested in the party."

"Oh, well, I suppose it'll be okay. Brian said he was only going because I am." The words sounded nice, the way I said them so casually.

I looked at myself in her mirror and wondered how I would look in a frizzy perm. No, I didn't want to look like everyone else. My hair was straight and I had spent a fortune on a layered haircut.

"Brian?" Mom was surprised. "I can't keep up with you, Annie. One minute you're complaining that everyone's too old for you; then you're crazy about a boy almost two years older." She shook her head.

"Oh, well, *c'est la vie*," I said, pleased with the chance to use the one French expression I knew.

Mom kept shaking her head.

"You look beautiful," said my dad the next night when I was ready to walk over to Caroline's. Of course he's my father and he would say that, but I did think I looked pretty neat. My hair was nice and shiny, the lavender blouse looked good against my suntan, and the earrings were just right.

The minute I walked in I saw that Brian was there. He was standing with his hands in his pockets looking uncomfortable. I had been thinking about him so much that I felt I knew him well, which was weird, since I didn't. I would have liked to go over and talk to him, but I didn't because he hardly looked at me. Caroline put on some records and everyone sat around talking. Sheila Kelly, who was in Caroline's homeroom, and Caroline were the only two girls the boys paid attention to. I watched them without being obvious. They knew what to do. They laughed, wrinkled up their noses, and flirted. It was very discouraging. I knew I couldn't behave that way.

The birthday cake and ice cream were served early because Caroline's parents were going out. I think they had to stop in at some friends' twenty-fifth wedding anniversary party. When her parents left, everything happened exactly as I knew it would. Caroline put out the lights, and everyone disappeared. I saw Brian going into the den, holding Sheila's hand.

I was alone in the living room. I felt I had become enormous, like Alice in Wonderland, when I wanted to be the size of a dormouse. I felt sick and headed for the bathroom. I knew Caroline's house as well as my own, but it was dark and I made a mistake and opened the door to her parents' room, which was next to the bathroom. Caroline and Ken were on the bed and they jumped apart when the door opened.

"Annie," Caroline shrieked. "What do you want?"

"I made a mistake. I thought I was going into the bathroom." I think I was stuttering.

"You know where the bathroom is. You're spying on me! I never should have invited you."

I closed the bedroom door and went into the bathroom. I sat down on the edge of the bathtub and cried. I knew Caroline was no longer my best friend.

Sometime later on, Caroline whispered that she was sorry. She said I had scared her, that she thought her mother had come home; but I knew our lives were going in different directions.

It was just about that time, perhaps the day after the party, that I decided I wanted to be a pianist, but I kept my feelings to myself. When my mother asked me on Sunday if I'd had a good time at the party, I told her it had been wonderful. "Did Brian walk you home?" she asked.

I had walked the short distance from Caroline's house to ours alone, but I thought Mom would be happy to think that Brian had been with me. "Yes, he did," I lied; "he was very nice."

"You kids grow up too soon these days," Mom said. "My little girl will be going out on dates before I know it. But not yet, Annie, don't grow up too fast."

"I'll try not to," I said, "but my friends want me to be with them."

Mom sighed. "Yes, I know, you don't want to be different. Sometimes I worry that it was a mistake for you to be thrown in with kids older than you. At your age I suppose it can make a difference."

"Don't worry about me, Mom, I'm fine." My voice was cheerful, but I turned away. She would never know that her daughter was a social flop.

2

As usual, the first day of school was hectic. Everyone was trying to straighten out their programs and no one knew where to go. In the halls people kept bumping into each other with lost, frantic expressions on their faces. Yet that very first day when I saw Miss Jones I knew she was different and special.

She was in the music room and while there wasn't a music class that day, she had put up a sign on her door that said, "Come in and get acquainted."

She was at the windows clearing some shelves, and she turned around when I said, "Hello."

13

She didn't look like a teacher at all. Her hair was long and blondish, and it was tied back with a ribbon. She was wearing a black turtleneck with an orange Mexican jumper over it. She was small, I guess what you'd call petite.

"Hello," she said. Her smile was shy, as if she weren't quite sure what to expect. She looked so young that I wondered if this was her first teaching job. It wasn't, and I found out later she wasn't as young as she looked. She was at least twenty-six, I think.

"I want to get rid of this stuff," she said, pointing to a bunch of old papers and magazines piled on the shelves. "I thought it would be nice to put some plants here; the room is so bare."

"That would be wonderful. Mr. Anderson, our music teacher last year, hung some posters on the walls, but I guess he took them with him. I could bring you some plants, if you'd like. I have a big garden and I have to do some transplanting."

She smiled. "That would be lovely. What is your name?"

"I'm Annie Kruger. Are we going to have instruments to play?"

"I hope so. We're going to do a lot of things. Maybe some things you haven't done before.

I'm very excited about working in this school because I was told I could be as creative as I wanted. What do you play?"

"I play the piano, and not very well. But I think I want to be a pianist."

"Good for you. Do you like classical music or rock?"

"I don't know much classical."

"Then we'll have to play some. Mozart, Brahms, Beethoven. You'll like it. In the beginning you may think it's old-fashioned, but it's not."

I thought of knights and ladies-in-waiting and houses with great halls and towers and turrets: myself dressed in a long gown, slender and beautiful, playing the piano.

I was lost in my daydream. "Do you like the idea of learning good music?" she asked.

"Sure, it sounds super. I was thinking we could do something with costumes. Like the clothes you see in Shakespeare's plays."

"That's a good idea. I can see we're going to get along fine, Annie Kruger. You have a nice imagination."

I thought about that conversation much later—that first conversation Miss Jones and I had. Neither of us knew then that my "imagination"—my mother said that was a kind word for it, and I suppose it was—was going to turn into something ugly. I never dreamed that a little story—I used to make up so many— would snowball and lead to such a big hullaba-loo.

When I came home from school that first day, Mom was there for a change. She worked in a bookstore in the village, and sometimes the owner's wife came in and Mom could go home early. She was trying on a jogging suit she had just bought. "How does it look?" she asked me.

"Okay." My mom was pretty but a little plump and I was glad she was going to take up jogging. "Do you know any music by Mozart, Brahms, or Beethoven?"

"What made you ask that?" She looked at me in surprise. "I know some."

"We have a super new music teacher and she's going to teach me to play classical mu-sic."

Mom was fussing with her new suit, pulling it one way and another. "Good, I want you to go on with your music. We have the piano, and I've been thinking since Miss Allison left that you should take lessons again."

"Maybe Miss Jones gives piano lessons. I'd like to take them from her."

"We'll see." She was standing in front of the mirror trying to look thin. "I'm glad you have a music teacher you like. Are you going over to Caroline's?"

"No. I'm going to dig up some plants for Miss Jones. She wants to put some in her room."

Mom threw me one of her amused smiles. "She really made a hit with you, didn't she?"

"She's not like the rest of the teachers. I think she likes me. She said I had a nice imagination."

Mom laughed. "You can say that again."

Bringing the plants to school was not easy. I had potted them and put the pots into a box, but everyone on the bus wanted to know why I was taking them to school. It was a relief to get them to Miss Jones's room. "This is wonderful," she said. She was wearing the same black turtleneck but this time she had on a turquoise jumper. She looked super. I couldn't wait to get to my music class that afternoon.

I was not one of those kids who hated school; most of the time I liked it. Maybe this was because I was an only child and there wasn't a lot to do at home, especially in the winter when I couldn't garden, swim, or hike. I read a lot but you can't read all the time, and making up stories was fun, but Mom said I did too much daydreaming although she had no idea what I thought about. But that fall, just a year ago, it was different. The only class I looked forward to was music and that was because Miss Jones made it so interesting, and she liked me. There was a kind of bond between us right from the beginning. Part of it was that we both loved plants, gardening, and music, but I think there was something more.

Mom thought I was becoming a loner. Without Caroline, I guess I was. Caroline and I didn't have a fight; we just drifted apart. Or I should say she drifted from me. She and Sheila became close friends—so they could talk about their boyfriends, I suppose.

I decided that Miss Jones was a loner too. She didn't mingle much with the other teachers, and before I even got to know her better I felt that she led a private and quiet life. She seemed content; she wasn't mopey and she looked as if she was happy with her thoughts, which was similar to the way I felt.

That very first music class, I remember feeling that I had met someone who was going to be important, who had ideals that would inspire me. When she talked about music and what she hoped to do in the class I felt happy.

"Music is something we experience," Miss Jones said. She was perched on her desk and she had asked us to bring our chairs close in a semicircle around her. "When you hear me talk about creativity in music, I am talking about creative expression. But before you can be creative, you must be able to understand musical concepts. Each one of you should strive to develop your own potential. The possibilities are infinite."

She made it sound exciting. Her face was serious and intense, and when she looked toward me, I felt she was talking especially to me.

"Isn't she fabulous?" I said to Caroline after class.

"A little weird, if you ask me. I hope she doesn't give us a lot of work. I like music because it's such a snap."

"I think it sounds exciting." That may have been the first time I didn't automatically agree with Caroline. As a matter of fact I felt superior. Her reaction seemed so gross. I felt all the more that Miss Jones had been speaking directly to me, someone she knew would understand her.

When I got home from school that day, I was sorry to find Mary there. Mary is the woman who comes twice a month to do the heavy cleaning because Mom has a bad back. Usually I was glad to see Mary, she's fun to talk to, but that day I felt like being alone.

As soon as Mary had finished vacuuming the living room, I went in there and began playing the piano. I had hardly touched the keys all summer, but I was able to play a waltz I had learned and felt good about it.

"Do you ever feel that life is mysterious?" I asked Mary later when I was in the kitchen eating an apple and some cookies.

She looked at me steadily. I would have been hurt if she had laughed, but she said, "Life is what you make it, Annie. It can be wonderful and it can be terrible."

When Mary left I had the house to myself for about an hour before Mom came home. I took a recording of some Beethoven sonatas that belonged to my parents and played it on my stereo. My room's not very big, but I pushed my old fur rug and my two chairs against the wall and danced to the music. It wasn't really dancing. I just swayed to the music, trying to capture the rhythm and doing so made me feel closer to Miss Jones.

3

We had a lovely fall last year. The weather stayed warm and dry except for a frost sometime in October that killed the tomato plants, but I had managed to pick all the tomatoes before it happened. After that we had Indian summer, which I like best. It's like a consolation prize, a kind of present before it gets cold and gray.

One day in October I persuaded Caroline to go for a walk with me. We still saw each other since we were neighbors, although I knew we would never be close the way we used to be. Our houses are right next to a state park with wonderful trails. Caroline and I used to go there all the time, but now she usually wanted to walk to the village where the boys hung out. That one Saturday I persuaded her to come with me to the park.

"I'll make sandwiches for lunch," I told her on the phone that morning.

Caroline laughed. "You're bribing me."

"Of course. I'm no fool."

"The sandwiches better be good," Caroline said. "Meet you at twelve o'clock."

It felt like old times when Caroline and I climbed the hill to the park trail, and went over the fence to get inside the park. I felt good. Whenever we went into the park I had a sense of excitement, as if something unexpected might happen. I had nothing specific in mind—I didn't expect to see wild animals or anything like that, but I pretended I was venturing into strange country. The park was something like a preserve; there were no lawns or planted flowers; everything was wild.

I couldn't talk about any of this to Caroline—she would have thought I was nuts—but the park made me think of Miss Jones. She would like it here, I thought, and I wondered if we would ever go walking here together. If I could manage it, I decided we would. "This is my last free Saturday," I said to Caroline.

"Why? What are you going to be doing?"

"I'm going to take piano lessons with Miss Jones. We start next Saturday morning."

"I'm going to take ballet. Mom found a class for me on Thursday afternoons. I wouldn't take lessons on Saturday if you paid me."

"I don't mind. Not with Miss Jones. Don't you think she's wonderful?"

Caroline stopped walking. "You have a crush on her, don't you?"

"I don't know. I don't know what a crush is. I like her a lot. I think she's a very unusual person."

"Unusual is the right word. I don't know what she's talking about half the time. She's weird."

"She's not weird; she's just different. The minute anyone's different, they're called weird. She makes me feel good. She thinks our world is too materialistic."

"How do you know that?"

"She talks to me sometimes. I think she's lonely, although she says she likes to be alone. I'm helping her take care of her plants, and when I have a free period I go into her room.

"Caroline, if I ask you something, will you tell me the truth?"

"Depends on what you ask." Caroline looked wary.

"Do you and Ken kiss a lot?"

Caroline looked relieved. "Sure we kiss. Haven't you ever kissed a boy?"

"No, and I don't think I want to. It must be yucky."

"Is that one of the ideas you got from your Miss Jones?"

"Oh, no. We never talk about anything like that. But I bet she isn't kissing any men."

"Then she ought to be a nun," Caroline said.

"She's kind of like a nun. . . . I don't know any nuns, but I imagine that's what they're like. Someone who believes in beauty and truth."

Caroline laughed. I must have looked hurt because she quickly said, "I'm not laughing at you, but you don't look the least bit ethereal. What you were saying doesn't seem to fit."

I looked down at my brown legs. I saw a Band-Aid on one knee where I'd scratched myself, not very clean shorts, and dirty tennis shoes. I had to laugh too. "But my heart is very pure," I said. "I am a saint in disguise. Tra-la-la . . ."

I was being silly, but Caroline said, "I hope not."

We had turned around and were on our way home when we saw someone coming toward us on a bike. We thought it was one of the girls from high school, but as the bike drew nearer we were both stunned to see it was Miss Jones.

Miss Jones seemed pleased to see us. "Isn't it a glorious day to be out? I'm glad to have met up with you two. I'm looking for the gorge. I was told it was beautiful, but I don't know if I missed the path to it or not." She was sitting on the bike, her feet resting on the ground. If she hadn't looked so serene, she would have looked like a kid.

"It's back further," I said, gesturing in the direction we had come from. "You haven't gone far enough."

"I hope I find it." She balanced herself on the bike.

"Would you like me to show you? It's easy to miss if you don't know it." I looked from her to Caroline.

"You go," Caroline said. "I'd better go home."

"If you really want to . . ." Miss Jones looked at me hesitantly.

"I'd love to. But you can't take a bike down the path to the gorge. It's narrow and very steep and rocky."

"Couldn't I just hide the bike in the bushes? I don't think anyone would take it." She laughed. "I don't want to go home without seeing the famous gorge."

"I suppose you could." I was dubious, but it was her bike and her decision.

We said good-bye to Caroline, and Miss Jones walked the bike alongside me. "You're very trusting," I said.

"I am. Most people are good."

When we got to the path, we buried her bike under a bunch of leaves and brush, and I led her down the trail. The gorge is very dramatic. A stream cuts through the state park, and at the gorge it becomes swift and tumbles over a thirty-foot cliff, making a powerful and spectacular waterfall. "In the summertime we sometimes try to stand under the waterfall," I told her. "It's sharp."

"You have a good time living here, don't you?"

"Sometimes. I don't have a lot of friends." We sat down on the grass.

"Neither do I. So we have that in common." She smiled at me. "A person doesn't need a lot of friends. You can enjoy many things alone. As a matter of fact, to walk in the woods alone can be more interesting than when you're with someone else. You see and hear more."

After a few minutes she got up to leave and we climbed back up the path. When we had dug out her bike, she turned to leave and said, "Annie, you're a nice girl. I'm glad I met you today. Thank you for showing me the gorge. Maybe sometime we can do it again."

I watched her ride away and then walked slowly along the path toward home. I was more aware of the sounds in the woods, and noticed the wild flowers along the path.

When I got home my parents were getting dressed to go out. I assured them that I didn't mind being alone. "I'll enjoy it," I said. Mom said there was dinner for me in the fridge, and I looked forward now to having the house to myself.

"Will you watch TV?" Mom asked.

"Probably not. Most likely I'll play some music." I told her about meeting Miss Jones in the park. "We're going to be friends," I said. "She said she wanted to be friends with me."

"That's very nice, but I'm sure Miss Jones has her own friends and her own life."

Mom finished pinning up her hair and put on some makeup.

"Miss Jones doesn't use makeup. She's beautiful the way she is."

"Young people are," Mom said, pressing a tissue against her lips. "It's when you get older that you think about using makeup."

"You're not old, Mom. Anyway, you look great."

"Thank you." She studied me for a minute. "You sure you'll be all right? You don't mind staying alone?"

"I don't mind, honest." I was going to repeat what Miss Jones had said about being alone, but I didn't want to. I wanted to keep that to myself.

4

Saturday morning I put on a new pair of jeans and a new striped T-shirt. I was ready to go for my piano lesson hours before it was time.

"I'm glad to see you so interested in your music," Dad said at breakfast.

"That's what a good teacher does. I'm eager to meet your Miss Jones; I wish you had more teachers you were enthusiastic about." Mom served the three of us scrambled eggs and bacon.

"She's different. She's not like a regular teacher. You'll see when you come for parents' conference."

After breakfast I was too restless to hang around the house so I told Mom I was going to walk around until it was time to go for my lesson. "You'll have quite a wait," Mom said, glancing at the clock. It wasn't nine yet and my lesson wasn't until ten.

"I don't mind. I feel like getting out."

Naturally I thought about Miss Jones while I walked. I was anxious to see her apartment, which she had told me was in a big, old-fashioned Victorian house that had been converted into apartments.

Her house was in an old part of the town. Long ago it had been an elegant neighborhood. It was a long walk from our house but it was a beautiful day so I enjoyed it. I hadn't been in that neighborhood in ages, but I liked it. The houses were nicer than the newer ones. They had big porches and gables; some even had towers. The streets were lined with huge old trees, and while some of the houses needed a painting, the street still looked elegant. Just the right place for Miss Jones to live.

One thing spoiled her block. At the corner there was a market, not a big supermarket, but a dingy-looking grocery store that didn't seem to belong. I walked past her house, Number 39, and then around the block several times. It didn't seem that it would ever be ten o'clock and I was beginning to feel stupid walking around. When I came back to her street for about the hundredth time, she was coming out of the grocery store carrying two big brown bags.

I ran over to her. "Hi. I was just on my way for my lesson." I reached out to take one of the grocery bags from her. "I can carry one."

"You can take the smaller one if you want. Thanks a lot. You're early, aren't you? I thought I'd get some shopping done before you got here."

It seemed peculiar for her to be shopping. That sounds silly, I know, but I didn't think of a teacher doing ordinary things, especially Miss Jones. A teacher was someone you only saw at school and it was hard to imagine a teacher doing things outside of school like other people.

Miss Jones's apartment was on the first floor. It went from the front to the back of the house. It was the nicest place I'd ever been in. The living room was in the front. It was painted white and had a very high ceiling; a big fireplace was at one end. She didn't have much furniture; she said she liked a lot of space. The piano took up part of the room, and she had a small sofa, upholstered in white, and a couple of chairs, and lots of big, fat cushions in bright colors on the floor. The bedroom was in the back and in the middle there was a tiny kitchen and a bathroom. "The best part," she said, "is that my landlady said I could have a garden in the backyard. I can't wait for spring so I can plant things."

I was watching her put away her groceries and I felt that we could be sisters. I imagined us living together, gardening, playing music, and going on hikes. It would be wonderful.

"There," she said, putting away a box of Cheerios.

"My favorite cereal," I said, making a mental note to tell Mom to buy some.

Miss Jones started my lesson by playing something for me. I loved the piece, which sounded wistful and sad.

Then Miss Jones asked me to try a simple piece. "You have good hands," she said; "they're strong and sensitive. If you practice, you should do well." I was thrilled.

I hated to leave when my lesson was over. I wished I could think of some reason to stay. I thought of asking her if she wanted to go to the park in the afternoon, but I felt shy. Then she said, "I have two tickets for a concert this afternoon, chamber music, but I don't suppose you'd be interested in that."

I was ashamed to say I didn't know what chamber music was, and I wasn't sure whether she was inviting me or not. I just looked at her and felt stupid.

But she understood what I was thinking. "Chamber music usually consists of a few strings, possibly a flute or an oboe, sometimes a piano," she explained. "I think of it as softer, more gentle music than that played by a full orchestra." She looked at me as if she were trying to decide something. "I suppose you have a lot of things to do on a Saturday afternoon?"

I shook my head. "I haven't. I haven't anything to do. Saturdays are usually boring."

"There's no reason ever to be bored, Annie. There is so much to see and do. Would you like to come to this concert with me? I'm not sure you'll like it . . . but it would be a good experience."

She had no idea how excited I was. "I'd love to go, that is if you really want me. I'd have to ask my mother."

"Yes, of course. It's just a little after eleven now. Why don't you go home and ask your mother and call me back. Here's my number."

She wrote it out on a slip of paper. "If you can go I'll pick you up a little before two-thirty. The concert's at three over at the Congregational church."

She was facing the window and the sun hit her face, and made her eyes the brightest blue. I couldn't believe that she wanted me to be her friend. I ran all the way home with the piece of paper in my pocket.

Mom was surprised by the invitation. "That's nice of her to ask you." She looked at me curiously. "You sure you want to go? It's not rock, you know."

"Oh, Mom." Someday she would realize that I was a serious person. That was one thing Miss Jones talked about a lot: "You have to be serious about what you are doing. Most people are afraid to be serious. In music, for example, they won't listen to Bach because they have to pay attention. They just want background music that doesn't demand anything."

Sitting next to Miss Jones in the church I tried concentrating on the music. They weren't playing Bach; they played Beethoven and Mozart. But my mind kept wandering. I wondered what Miss Jones was thinking about. Some of the time she listened with her eyes closed. She looked as though she had a secret that made her happy. Having been in her house that morning, having first met her marketing and then watched her put away her groceries, made me feel close to her. Now I wanted to know all about her, what she did, what she thought about. I imagined how wonderful it would be if she invited me home for supper. We could eat in front of the fireplace and talk. For that I'd give up the TV show I watched on Saturday nights in a minute. As a matter of fact, I made up my mind right then and there I wasn't going to waste my time watching that silly TV show anymore.

When we left the church Miss Jones asked if I'd mind stopping at the Country Wood Stove shop. "They have a sale on wood stoves," she said. "I've been thinking of putting a wood stove in the fireplace and saving on oil. Today's the last day of the sale."

"I don't mind at all," I said.

The young man who waited on us said, "This can do more than heat one room." We were looking at a pretty, old-fashioned stove that I hoped she would buy. "If you put this in a room that had doors to other rooms and you left them open, it could heat several rooms."

"I don't have a very big apartment," Miss Jones said. "I live alone."

"This would be perfect for you. It's easy to take care of." I glanced up, and saw the salesman looking at Miss Jones in a way that made me feel he had forgotten about both me and the stove. Miss Jones must have felt it too, for she lowered her eyes and said in a soft voice, "I think I'd like to have it."

He was quite a bit taller than she, and I have to admit, good-looking. That is, if you like that kind of looks, very strong, dark, with thick black hair, Italian-looking. "I don't suppose you can deliver it until Monday," she said. "I don't get home until late Monday because I have meetings after school. . . ."

He asked her where she lived, and when she gave him her address his face broke into a wide grin. "That's not far from where I live, just a few blocks away. I'll be glad to bring it over when I leave here. We close at six; will you be home then?"

"That's very kind of you, but I don't want to impose," she murmured.

"It's no imposition. I could set it up for you; it has to be connected to the flue."

"That would be wonderful." She smiled and he looked down at her as if she were a kitten he wanted to pet. I didn't know it, but I had just met Mr. Jason Pascal who, in a way, was to be the cause of all my trouble.

I say I didn't know it, yet I think I did know. Just watching them I knew that something had happened. I'm no psychic, and perhaps because of what happened later I only think I knew it then. One thing I can say is that right from the beginning I didn't like him. Later, when he started calling for Miss Jones at school and Caroline and the other girls saw him, they said how sexy he was. I thought he was gross. He just didn't belong with Miss Annabel Jones: He was so *physical* and she was so *spiritual*.

She made out a check to him and we left. She was very quiet on the way home and dropped me off at my house. I kept thinking about her going home and his coming over. She had stopped to buy a bottle of wine and I wondered if she were going to offer him some. I kept wishing she had asked me home for supper. As a matter of fact, I was wishing it so hard, and thinking about it so much, that I told my mother that she had invited me. It made me feel good to say it out loud.

Mom frowned. "She must be lonesome. Doesn't she have any friends here?"

"Maybe she likes me," I said.

"You're just a young girl, Annie. Miss Jones is a teacher. . . . I'm sure she likes you but you're not a suitable companion for her."

"We get along very well; we talk about a lot of things."

"Maybe I should invite her for dinner sometime. Not that we'd be right for her; she needs friends her own age."

I thought of Mr. Pascal, who was about her age. But I didn't think he was right for her either. "Mom, *will* you invite her for dinner?"

"I'll have to meet her first. I'll see when we go to parents' conference."

5

One Sunday a couple of weeks later I was roller-skating with Caroline. She was telling me a lot of stuff I really wasn't interested in: "I think Sheila's jealous of Ken and me," Caroline said, "because she broke up with her boyfriend. Actually I think she wishes Ken and I would break up and then she could go with Ken. But she doesn't stand a chance. Ken doesn't even like her."

It sounded silly and boring. Going with a boy meant a lot of kissing and stuff. They didn't really *go* anywhere except to a basketball or soccer game, and they passed a lot of notes around in school and giggled a lot. "Well, I don't have to worry about anyone taking a boyfriend away from me. I'm glad I don't have a boyfriend." I tried a quick turn on my skates.

"Maybe that's sour grapes," Caroline said.

"I knew you'd say that, but it isn't."

We skated down to the end of our road and turned around. "You're different," Caroline said. "You're not even the way you used to be. You're so hung up on Miss Jones. She's okay but you can't have fun with a teacher."

"But we do have fun. You probably wouldn't think so. We play music and she gives me books to read. We talk a lot." I didn't tell Caroline that she gave me books of poetry to read. She'd have really thought that weird. "I think Miss Jones thinks boyfriends are silly too. That is, until you're old enough to be truly in love and ready to get married."

"She's old enough. She could get married if she wanted to."

I knew that. And once in a while I thought about it. What if Miss Jones met someone and fell in love? I wouldn't mind if it was someone I liked. We could still be friends—perhaps even better friends. If she and her husband went on camping trips I could go with them—Miss Jones said that she loved to go camping and wished she had the right person to go with. A husband would be the right person, and I wouldn't be any trouble. I could gather wood for a fire, and I was pretty good at making bacon and eggs. I could be a help, since I knew a lot about the woods and wild flowers. My mind raced on and I had almost forgotten about Caroline skating a little ahead of me, when Brian came along on his bike.

"Hi," he said and stopped to watch us skate. Then he said, "Want to go for a bike ride?"

I wasn't looking at him. "Go ahead," I said to Caroline, "I don't mind."

"He asked you, dopey," she said.

I turned around, and there was Brian, his hair falling over his forehead, his round face pink from the wind, looking at me.

"Where are you going?"

"To the park, I guess. That's the best place to ride."

I looked from him to Caroline. "Go ahead." I don't know why she whispered it since Brian could hear her perfectly well.

"Okay, I'll get my bike."

I wasn't keen on going; I felt nervous. But I didn't know how to say no. I couldn't think of an excuse fast enough, and Caroline would have thought I was silly. We crossed the road into the park and rode on the path, side by side. I couldn't think of a thing to say. And with Brian glancing over at me, I couldn't enjoy my own thoughts. I got mad at myself for being such a jerk. I was never going to be one of those ass-wiggling, giggling girls who played up to a boy: Brian had asked me to go for a ride; if he wanted to talk, let *him* think of what to talk about.

We rode in silence for what seemed like ninety hours until we came to the path leading down to the gorge. "Let's park our bikes and climb down," Brian said. The last thing I wanted to do was to go down to the gorge with him, but it was better than riding along in silence.

At first it was fun. Brian kicked stones down, and then I kicked some. Soon we had a game going: whose stone would roll the farthest.

When we got to the bottom of the waterfall Brian made believe he was running through the water, but he was actually hiding among the rocks. We were having a good time when two people came climbing down the path. I was stunned to see it was Miss Jones and Mr.

Pascal. She was just as surprised to see us. I think she was embarrassed. "Jason, I want you to meet two of my pupils," she said, introducing Mr. Jason Pascal to Brian and me. He was carrying a little knapsack that he took off his back and put on a rock; they had a picnic with them. He had on a running suit; Miss Jones wore a sweatshirt, slacks, and hiking shoes. I'd never seen her in casual clothes before. She looked different, and he kept calling her Annabel, which made everything even odder. After all, they had only met a few weeks before—*I* had been there to see it—and here they were having a picnic and calling each other by their first names.

Mr. Pascal turned to Brian. "I'm starving," he said. "Would you like to help me get some wood for a fire?"

"Sure." He and Brian clambered off the rocks in search of wood. My anger was rising. It was unreasonable, I knew, but I took an intense dislike to Mr. Pascal, and I was furious with Brian for being friendly.

"Jason is a musician too," Miss Jones said. It was as though she knew how much I hated him. "He plays the saxophone. Very well, too."

"I thought he worked in that stove store."

"He does; he has to pay his rent. Unfortunately a musician cannot always make a living with his music. He doesn't plan to sell wood stoves forever. I'm sorry we don't have enough food for you and Brian," she added. She was laying a cloth on the rocks and taking bags of food out of the knapsack.

"That's okay. We have to go anyway." I wanted Brian to get back so we could leave. I didn't want to have a picnic with Miss Jones and him. "How's the stove doing?" I asked, just to say something. A dumb question since I saw the stove when I went for my lessons.

"It's terrific. I love it."

"The fireplace was prettier." I thought I saw a smile cross her face. She could laugh; I suppose I was being ridiculous, but finding her here with Mr. Pascal was a shock.

She didn't know how much I thought about her, and how I always imagined her being alone. When I thought of her this way I didn't mind being alone myself. It was as though her aloneness made mine okay.

When Mr. Pascal and Brian got back I told Brian I wanted to leave. When we got to the top of the gorge, I sat down on a rock. "Tired?" Brian asked.

"No. I just feel like sitting for a while." He sat down on the grass, and picked up blades he could whistle through. A lot of thoughts were going through my mind.

"What made you ask me to go for a bike ride?" I asked.

Brian shrugged. "I don't know. Just felt like it. You didn't have to come if you didn't want to."

"I know. It's just that I don't think you like me very much."

He grinned. "Maybe I do and maybe I don't. What makes you think I don't?"

"You haven't tried to kiss me."

He shot me a wary glance. "Did you want me to?"

"I don't know. I just thought it was what boys did."

"I can kiss you if you want." He came over and sat against my legs. "Bend down."

"No." I thought he should sit up—at least put his arm around me. The whole thing seemed stupid, and I was about to stand when Brian slid up onto the rock and leaned over and kissed me. It happened very fast, and I think he was as surprised as I. There was a big grin on his face. "It didn't hurt, did it?"

"No worse than a mosquito bite." We both laughed uproariously.

On the way back Brian said, "You don't like boys much, do you?"

"What makes you think I don't?"

"The way you act. You don't fool around the way other girls do."

"I'm not like other girls." As far as I was concerned the kiss had been pretty flat. I wasn't about to explain to Brian that I considered all that stuff gross, and that a meeting of the minds was what was truly important between people. He wouldn't have understood.

When I got home I went up to my room. I sat by the window and stared at the sky, but I couldn't empty my mind. Thoughts kept creeping in. I kept thinking about Miss Jones and Mr. Jason Pascal sitting at the gorge. I wondered if he was going to kiss her. When people kissed in a TV movie it wasn't anything like what Brian and I had done. Would Miss Jones and Mr. Pascal kiss the way they did on TV? It was a disgusting thought.

The next day in school Miss Jones looked the same as always in her Mexican jumper, with her scrubbed face and Indian earrings. It was a relief. I figured she had probably just been polite to Mr. Pascal because he had installed her stove. It never occurred to me that they had probably been seeing each other right along. In class we talked about a music festival that she wanted to put on in the spring. Every day for a week there would be a different event: one day a jazz concert, another a classical recital, then a day of choral music, and so forth. And on Friday night at the end of the week, there would be a concert for parents and friends. Even Caroline thought it sounded neat.

Everything was going great until Thursday. When I came into music class that day I noticed right away that Miss Jones looked different. It took me awhile to figure out why. Then I realized she was wearing high heels instead of her usual flat sandals, and that she had on eye makeup and lipstick. I didn't like it; it made her look ordinary.

That day I stayed after school to watch a basketball game and when we came out it was a little after five. Mr. Pascal was waiting in his car for Miss Jones. That explained everything. I suppose it sounds stupid for a kid to be jealous of a teacher (jealousy is what Mom called it later), but I wasn't exactly jealous of him. It was her having a boyfriend that depressed me. With her as an example I hadn't been bothered by Caroline and Sheila and their talk about boys. I felt special, separate, and above all that. But now Miss Jones was failing me.

I watched her get into the car. Mr. Pascal leaned over and kissed her.

I stopped to put into my briefcase a book of poems by Edna St. Vincent Millay that Miss Jones had given me; it was either that or drop it into a garbage can. I didn't want to read her book.

That night when I got into bed I thought about Brian. I wished he had given me a real kiss; I wanted to know what it was like. Caroline and Sheila whispered a lot and I knew the important things—how babies are born and that stuff—but I didn't know what kids my age did when they were alone. And I wondered what Miss Jones and Mr. Pascal did when they were alone.

I felt restless. I tossed and turned and couldn't find a comfortable place in my bed. For a few minutes I thought of going to Mom. I wanted to be held and hugged. My body felt sweaty, so I got up and washed my face with cold water. That made me feel a little better, and I went back to bed and tried to think of other things. I thought about going swimming and playing tennis and of picnics on the beach. I was ashamed of my darker thoughts.

6

Parent-teacher conferences came after Halloween. Mom had met Miss Jones once for a couple of minutes when she had picked me up from my music lesson. "She looks interesting," Mom had said, but that was all I could get out of her.

"What are you going to wear?" I asked Mom, the night she was coming to school with me to meet my teachers.

She looked surprised. "My blue suit, I guess. What difference does it make what I wear?" She had an amused smile.

"I want to show you off." I said it jokingly, but it was true. Mom and I are close in some ways, and miles apart in others. If you haven't noticed, my dad isn't in this story at all. The reason is, he's hardly ever home. He's sales manager for a big chain of retail stores and he's always on the road. It makes Mom unhappy and I think it's lousy, but Dad says he can't change jobs now. It seems to me he's been saying that for years. I feel as if I hardly know him. So Mom and I are home together a lot, but Mom won't talk about private things. If I ask her if she misses Dad, she says, "Of course." But that's all. She won't say what she's really feeling.

Once last summer I came into the living room unexpectedly and she was curled up in front of the TV crying.

"What's the matter?" I asked.

"Nothing. Just a silly story." But a dumb travelogue was on and I knew that couldn't have made her cry.

Since she won't talk to me about anything important, I don't feel I can talk to her. We talk about food and clothes, stuff like that, but not much more. She had no idea how nervous I was about her meeting Miss Jones. I wanted her to look her best, but I was also wishing she were the kind of person who could get close to Miss Jones, because that would make me closer too. But I knew that couldn't happen.

Mom has friends, but I'm not sure she's close to anyone.

When we got to school we had to go to my homeroom first; our appointment with Miss Jones was the last. We had to see all of the other teachers before going to the music room. Miss Jones had told me she was very anxious to meet my mother, and when we came into her room she gave us a warm greeting.

"It's been a pleasure working with Annie," she said, "both here in the classroom and in her private lessons. I enjoy every minute of it, and I hope she does too."

It was embarrassing listening to her. They talked about music for about five minutes, and then it was over.

I don't know what I expected, but that was a letdown. It was very impersonal. Miss Jones could have been talking about anyone.

"Isn't she nice?" I asked Mom when we left her room.

"She seems pleasant."

"Is that all you have to say?" I was irritated. Not with Mom, but it came out that way.

Mom laughed. "You really have a crush on her."

"I do not." I lied. "What is a crush, anyway?"

"A brief infatuation. You'll get over it. Soon you'll be going out with boys and you'll forget about Miss Jones."

I will never forget her, I thought to myself. And I will probably not go out with boys either—although it had occurred to me that I should find out more about boys so I would know what I was giving up.

Mr. Pascal's car was in front of the school. I hadn't seen him for the past few weeks and I had decided that Miss Jones must have stopped seeing him. But there she was, going over to him with an eager smile on her face. She got in beside him and leaned over for a kiss as if it were something she did all the time. She probably did.

"You didn't tell me Miss Jones had a boy-friend," Mom said. "I was feeling sorry for her being all alone in a new town."

"I don't know if he's her boyfriend."

"They look pretty close." Miss Jones was snuggling up next to him. "I'm glad for her. A young woman her age should have someone. She's attractive, too."

"She doesn't believe in that stuff," I said. "She's not like other people."

Mom had gotten into our car and I sat down beside her. She frowned and said, "Don't romanticize Miss Jones. She may be sensitive but I am sure she wants to lead a normal life, the way most women do . . . the way you will too when you get older."

"I don't want to talk about it."

Mom didn't say anything more, and we had an uncomfortable ride home. When we were in the kitchen Mom acted as if everything were okay. Mom was that way. She could say something important, or upsetting, and then go right on as if she hadn't said it. "You want some cocoa?" she asked.

"No, I think I'll go to bed." She looked disappointed and started to put the milk back in the refrigerator. "Okay, if you want some. Do you want me to make it?"

"No, you can cut some of the cake that's left."

I knew she was lonely. I guess the way Mom and Dad lived made me feel cool toward marriage. Even when Dad was home you'd have thought they'd be together every minute, but they weren't. Mom went to work; Dad went to his office. She went shopping on Saturday and he'd spend all day making something in his workshop. Sunday he'd read the newspapers and Mom would cook and bake, and ask me to go for a walk because Dad hardly ever wanted to. It was hard to imagine they had ever been in love.

One week in November we had a streak of unusually warm weather. When I came home from school on those days I put on my old jeans and a sweater and worked outside. There were still leaves to be raked and the fall mess in the garden to be cleaned up. It was wonderful to have sunny weather to do it in and I enjoyed myself. It was supposed to turn cold on the weekend, so I worked like a beaver on Friday to finish. I was putting a last batch of leaves on the compost heap when Brian appeared. He sat on a bench at our picnic table and said, "I like to watch you work."

"Sure, while you loaf. Come on, help me fold this tarp up. And you came right in time to put the wheelbarrow down in the cellar for me."

"I said I liked to watch *you* work."

"I thought that's what you said." He had picked up the other end of the tarp. "We fold it this way." We walked toward each other, each holding an end of the big tarp, and when we met, Brian gave me a quick kiss. Although I felt I should say he was fresh, I smiled.

When we were finished, Brian came into the

kitchen with me. While I was getting us each a soda and some cookies, he was squirming around like a puppy with fleas. "I've been thinking about what you said when we went on the bike ride," he said finally.

"I said a lot of things."

"I mean about boys kissing girls. Do a lot of boys kiss you?"

I laughed. "Millions."

"I'm serious. I'd like to know." He drank his soda from the bottle, but I poured mine into a glass.

"I don't think it's something one talks about, but I'll tell you anyway. No boys kiss me."

Brian looked pleased. "That's good." He came over to me and put his arm around me. "I'm going to kiss you."

I was going to push him away, but then I changed my mind: I would never learn anything if I didn't start somewhere. Besides, I wanted him to. His arms around me tightened and he kissed me. I threw my arms around him and we kissed again, and again. . . .

Then he ran out of the kitchen without even saying good-bye. I didn't finish my soda or eat any cookies. I sat in the kitchen feeling shaky. Waves of shame swept over me. Never again would I let a boy kiss me. Not because of anything Brian had done, but because of me. I had wanted to go on kissing, to have him hold me, to touch me. . . . I was the one who was gross and disgusting. I had betrayed all the ideals Miss Jones had given me. After my last lesson we had sat and talked, and she had said, "The people who lead an ascetic life are the happiest. Monks and nuns, certain religious persons in India and the East—those who have given up physical comfort and physical gratification, they lead lives that are free. Free of ambition and of disappointment, free of emotional discontent." She had sighed and added, "I wish I could be like them. Life would be so uncomplicated. . . ."

She could be like that. I forgot about Mr. Pascal, and thought that I could be that way too. But now I knew I was just as ordinary as Caroline and Sheila. I hated myself.

I was still in the kitchen when Mom came home. She saw the two soda bottles and asked who had been over.

"Brian helped me do a couple of things outside," I said.

"That was nice of him. You two are getting to be quite friendly, aren't you?" She had a sly smile on her face.

"No, we're not."

"I thought you liked him."

"I can't stand him," I lied. "He's a creep."

Mom gave me an anxious look. "Did he do something you didn't like? Get fresh?"

I was mortified. If she only knew how fresh her own daughter was. "No one can get fresh with me," I said. "I know how to take care of myself." I left the kitchen and went upstairs to take a shower.

7

On Saturday when I went for my piano lesson I hoped I'd have a chance to talk to Miss Jones. I noticed that her woodbox was empty and when the lesson was over I offered to bring in wood for her. "That would be very nice, Annie," she said.

When I had her box filled to the top and saw that she was relaxing, certainly not acting as if she were in a hurry to do something, I said, "Can I talk to you a minute?"

She gave me her smile. "Sure."

I was nervous about what I wanted to say. "I know you know a lot, but if you're just a kid, how do you keep from thinking bad thoughts and having bad feelings?"

"I'm not sure that you do, even when you're not a kid. I don't know what bad thoughts you mean, but most people have some wicked thoughts. And maybe some of the things you think are bad are just natural—thoughts that most girls your age have." Her face flushed and I think she was embarrassed. "Sometimes we try to convince ourselves we can do without things just because we haven't got them, like trying to forget about food when there's nothing to eat. Don't be afraid of your feelings, Annie."

She wasn't saying what I wanted to hear. I didn't want to be like "most girls"—I wanted her to help me get rid of the thoughts I had about Brian. I didn't want to think about whether I was going to see him out in the yard when I went out. I wanted to enjoy being outside the way I used to. I didn't want to feel a pang of jealousy when I saw Caroline and Ken arm in arm. I didn't want to lie in bed at night thinking about Brian.

I felt let down. She was the only person who could help me, but all she was saying was that everything was all right. It wasn't, but I saw that I was going to have to handle it alone.

Mom had told me I could ask Miss Jones over for dinner if I wanted to, but not to make her feel obligated to come because I was her student. I didn't know how to manage that, but I asked her anyway. "That would be nice," she said. "I'd love to come." We set a date for the following week and I was about to leave, when Mr. Pascal came in. He didn't ring or knock, just walked in the front door. I suppose he had a key. He was carrying a bunch of flowers.

Miss Jones got a little fluttery. I think she was embarrassed. I left quickly, and it was only when I was outside that I thought about his having a key. Did that mean that he was living there? Thinking about it made me feel funny. I wanted to know more, yet I was ashamed. I decided he couldn't possibly be living there. She'd probably given him the key in case he had to come in to fix the stove or something while she was in school.

Miss Jones was coming to our house for dinner on Wednesday night, and I was excited that morning. I had tried to forget about Mr. Pascal. Miss Jones had been the same as always in school, so I figured nothing had changed. If she were in love I would have known—she wouldn't have been so fussy about our performance in music class, nor would she have talked about spiritual and aesthetic values so seriously. I didn't think kissing was especially spiritual or aesthetic. From what I had read, people behaved differently when they were in love.

After third period, I came back to homeroom and found a note on my desk. I opened it and read: *Brian loves Annie.* I read it again and turned crimson. Then I tore it up and threw it in the wastebasket. I was immediately sorry because I wanted to look at it some more. I had no idea who could have written it, and it made me feel queasy. I guessed someone was playing a joke on me, but why? I was sure Brian hadn't written it, yet when I wondered, What if he had? it made me nervous. I was afraid to look at him and afraid to see him again.

When I got home from school I stayed in the house all afternoon. I didn't want to go out in the yard for fear I'd see Brian. I saw him on his bike from my window and he looked the same as always, but I felt uncomfortable even looking at him from inside.

I thought about Miss Jones coming over and was glad that my dad was home. She came around six o'clock, and looked very pretty. I could tell my father thought she was pretty by the way he looked at her. Mom offered her a glass of white wine and they all had a drink while I passed the cheese.

At the table, Dad asked her about teaching music, and she spoke about the things she always talked about. "My aim is to get my students to experience the creative and aesthetic value of music," Miss Jones said. She spoke very earnestly. They talked a lot about music and teaching. I was worried that Mom and Dad would think she was weird but they seemed to think she was okay. She left soon after dinner, saying she had work to do. As soon as she was out the door I asked them how they had liked her.

"She seems like a nice young woman," Mom said.

"Is that all you have to say?"

"Don't expect me to go into ecstasies over a teacher," Mom said.

"She won't be a teacher for long," Dad said. "I'm surprised she's not married already."

"Miss Jones has no intention of getting married," I told them. "She's going to lead a spiritual life."

They both looked at me as if I were from

another planet. "You don't have to look at me that way. I know her better than you do. She has taken a vow of chastity," I said grandly.

"Annie, you don't know what you're talking about," Mom said sharply. "I don't know what kind of nonsense you and Miss Jones talk about, but I think you'd better stick to music."

Dad was laughing. "Your Miss Jones doesn't look so ethereal to me."

"You don't know her," I said coldly. I was not going to let Mr. Pascal or anyone else change my mind about Miss Jones. She was special and different, and whether they knew it or not I was going to be just like her.

I didn't know then what was in store for me but I found out the following Saturday when I went for my piano lesson. The minute I went into Miss Jones's apartment, I sensed that something was different. Usually everything was very neat: the chairs and pillows in the same place, the books on her table in an even pile, the magazines arranged in an orderly way. But that day newspapers were spread out all over the floor. It looked as if someone had been reading them and had just walked away and left them. The pillows were pushed up against the wall, magazines were scattered on the table. I saw a pipe sitting in an ashtray and knew immediately that Mr. Pascal had been there and made himself at home.

Miss Jones had on eye makeup and perfume—she'd never worn perfume before—and she acted as if her mind were someplace else. Twice I asked her about the way I was playing a piece and she looked blank and asked, "What did you say?"

Before I left I went into the bathroom, and then I knew. He was living there. His shaving stuff was on the shelf, and on the hooks behind the door a pair of men's blue pajamas hung next to her nightgown.

I sat down on top of the toilet seat to compose myself. I was in a state of shock. It was the most awful feeling I'd ever had: hurt, betrayed, confused. And then angry. She was sleeping with a man—she was gross and ordinary like everybody else. I cried over a loss I could not name.

Much later, Mom said, "But you are only twelve. You mustn't feel so desperate." That was when I told her a little about how I had felt. Not all—I couldn't tell anyone all. "You have a whole wonderful life ahead of you," Mom said. Perhaps. But on that day I would never have believed it.

I splashed cold water on my face, and went

out to say good-bye to Miss Jones. She looked the same as when I had come in but I knew she had changed. Her mind was full of ordinary things. I didn't believe she was musing anymore about a spiritual life, about the serenity of one's inner self—she was thinking about what to do with her hair, what to wear when she went out with him, if he loved her, and how much he loved her. All the things Caroline talked about day after day.

"Are you all right?" Miss Jones asked. She had his saxophone case in her hand and she caught me looking at it. "Jason's saxophone," she said, as if I didn't know. She gave me a questioning look. "You don't like him, do you?"

"I don't care one way or another." I didn't want to talk; I wanted to leave.

"One of these days you'll have a boyfriend, you'll see."

"I don't think I will. I don't intend to."

"It's a little early to make up your mind, Annie. Life isn't all black and white. You don't have to be absolutely one thing or another. You change, you grow, you have to be open. Things happen."

"I have to go home," I said.

But I didn't feel like going home so I went to

the park. I wanted to be alone to sort things out. What I couldn't get over was that Miss Jones had lied to me. She had made me believe that she was committed to living a different kind of life. I felt as if the bottom had fallen out of everything: I had been trying so hard to ignore my feelings about Brian. I had wanted to be like her, and now she had changed. I felt like a fool.

I walked past the path to the gorge but I didn't have the heart to go down it. It reminded me of her and of Brian. I walked some more and then turned to go back. On the way home Brian came along on his bike.

"Hi. What are you doing here by yourself?" Brian had on a red woolen cap and his cheeks were almost the same color.

"I just felt like walking."

"Want to go down to the gorge? I can park my bike."

"No, I don't feel like it."

"What's the matter? You mad at me?"

"No. Why should I be mad at you?"

"I don't know. I . . ." He got off his bike and leaned it against a tree and walked over to me. "You look pretty today. Sad but pretty." He leaned over and kissed me. "I like you," he said.

"Don't do that," I shouted. I ran down the path and cut into the woods. I stumbled over some twigs and fell onto a soft mound of moss. For the second time that day I burst into tears.

Brian knelt down beside me. "What's the matter?"

"Go away," I mumbled. "Leave me alone."

He stood up and I lifted up my head to see him. "Don't mind me. It has nothing to do with you." I was lying. I wanted him to go away and at the same time I wanted him to stay. I didn't know what I wanted. He looked at me for a few minutes and then he turned and walked away. I wanted to call him back but I couldn't. I just sat there.

After a while I went home. "How'd your lesson go?" Mom asked.

"Terrific," I said automatically.

"How's Miss Jones? Does she still have a boyfriend?"

"How should I know? Besides, I don't think he's her boyfriend. She's not interested in that kind of thing."

Mom gave me a curious look. "You look tired. Are you all right?"

"I'm fine." But I went to my room and stretched out on my bed. Why had I said that to Mom about Miss Jones? I didn't think I was a liar, yet I said things that weren't true because I wished that they were. Saying them somehow made them real. I thought I would have to stop doing that.

8

That winter was the worst of my life. Even the first snow, which came just before Christmas, did not excite me. It only made me feel sad. I don't think it was just Miss Jones and Mr. Pascal. They didn't help, though, since it was clear that he spent a lot of his time at Miss Jones's. I went on with my piano lessons and I practiced a lot. Once, on a very cold day after Christmas vacation, when my lesson was over Miss Jones asked if I wanted a cup of hot cocoa before I left.

"That would be nice," I said. Jason often came in at the end of my lesson but that day there was no sign of him.

When we sat at the table it seemed like old times. She talked about the spring music festival and her eyes sparkled. "How about playing a solo?" she asked. "I was thinking of one of the Mozart sonatas you've been practicing. Would you like that?"

"Do you think I could do it?"

"I think so. I'm sure you can, if you work hard between now and then." She gave me a beautiful smile.

"It makes me nervous thinking about a big audience."

"Don't think about it. You play well when you don't daydream."

"I know." I looked at her and wondered if she knew I daydreamed about her. "I like to daydream."

"We all do a little." She eyed me seriously. "How are you getting along, Annie? I notice you're alone a lot in school."

"You once said that we were both loners. And that you didn't mind being alone, you liked it."

She put down her cup and leaned back in her chair. "Did I say that?" She laughed. "Maybe I said it because I didn't have a friend then. Everyone needs someone. You'll see. You're probably going through a phase now. You need friends, Annie, and one of these days some boy will come along. . . ." She kept smiling. "You'll see."

I got up. "I have to go now." I didn't want to listen to her. Going through a phase! Was that what people did, go through phases, like studying American history one year and European the next? Wasn't there anything permanent and secure to hold on to?

When I got home I called up Caroline, but she was out. Mom wasn't home and Dad was away. I felt depressed, and sat in my room and moped.

That is my main impression of that winter, feeling depressed. I wasn't depressed all the time, though. I went ice-skating, and had a wonderful weekend in Vermont skiing with my Aunt Molly, and I went to the movies and a few parties. Mom bought me a bra, but I felt disconnected. My body was changing, developing the way it was supposed to, but the rest of me (whatever that rest is—the soul? the mind? the spirit?) was going nowhere.

I kept thinking that things would change when spring came, and something did happen, but it wasn't wonderful.

I remember coming out of school one day in late March and sniffing the air. It felt like spring. I knew we could still have plenty of cold weather, but soon it would be time to plant some peas and lettuce. I might even start some cold flats soon. I was going to walk into the village instead of taking the bus home, and walking ahead of me I saw Caroline and Ken together, holding hands, their arms swinging in rhythm. Watching them made me feel sad. It was like looking at the empty space on my shelf at home after Mom had thrown away my Raggedy Ann doll. That was a few years ago, but even now I sometimes look at that space and feel a sense of loss.

I was going to the village to buy Miss Jones a birthday present. A few months earlier it would have been a happy event. I love buying presents and giving them, and buying something for her would have been super. Her birthday was on Friday, but she said she was going to celebrate it on Saturday because Jason had plans. However, she invited me to have some birthday cake with them after my lesson on Saturday. Then she and Jason were going out.

I wasn't thrilled about being with them, but I said that I would. That's the way it had been right along. She was terrific when we rehearsed for the music festival, and when we were alone for my lesson it was the same. But the minute Jason appeared everything changed.

I didn't know what to buy her for a present. "Don't buy anything too personal," Mom had said.

"What's too personal?"

"Something to wear—it's hard to explain. You could buy her a book, or some cologne, or even a scarf, something like that."

None of those things appealed to me. I wanted to get something special but it had to be under ten dollars, five that I had saved up and five that I had borrowed from Mom. We only have two gift shops in Half-Mile Brook, and I went to one and then to the other and then back to the first. Finally I decided on a lovely enamel box. It was $10.95 but the lady let me have it for an even ten, and she wrapped it up in pretty paper and ribbon.

Saturday morning I put on my best skirt and blouse but I kept thinking how nice it would be if Miss Jones and I were going to a concert together the way we once had. But that was the day she had met Mr. Pascal. Out of my window I could see Brian in his yard shooting balls into his basketball net. He had grown over the winter and was better-looking, but I had been avoiding him. I didn't want to be alone with him. Every time I thought about Brian I hated

Mr. Pascal even more. It was as though he were to blame for my confusing feelings about Brian. Brian wasn't anything like Mr. Pascal but they both made me feel ambivalent about being alone.

Even though Miss Jones had changed, I was determined not to. I could see the difference and while she was still beautiful, she was more ordinary now. Even her clothes had changed. Now, on Saturdays, instead of wearing her exotic clothes, she wore jeans like everybody else and she talked about having to get her car washed and shopping for dinner and doing the laundry.

Miss Jones looked especially pretty on her birthday, even in ordinary clothes. She was wearing a blue silk blouse with a skirt. She had on makeup and her hair was up so she looked like a movie star.

She was anything but serene. First she sat down with me at the piano and then she got up, saying she had to take something out of the freezer. Then she had to make a telephone call. She was jumping around like a grasshopper. For the first time I couldn't wait to get the lesson over with. My mind kept wandering and I thought, What's so great about a piano lesson and listening to her say "more fortissimo," or "a little slower," or whatever. I could feel that she didn't care about it either. Her eyes kept looking toward the door and she kept smoothing her hair. And her perfume stank.

The lesson was almost over when Jason arrived carrying a big bunch of roses. He had on cowboy boots and a cowboy hat and she looked at him as if he were Robert Redford. "Am I too early? I couldn't think of anything else to do outside."

"No, it's okay." She took the roses from him. "They're gorgeous." She stood on her toes and kissed him. Then she turned to me. "You're staying for our party, aren't you, Annie?"

"If you still want me to."

"Of course we want you to. It's not going to be much of a party. . . ."

"That's all right," I said.

I should have gone home. I should have said I had to meet my mother; I should have known how angry I was, and how angry I was going to be. I didn't want to be with the two of them looking at each other the way they were.

Miss Jones put the roses in a vase in the middle of the round table, and they both disappeared into the kitchen. I could hear them giggling. When they came out, Jason was carrying a tray with a pitcher of martinis for them, a glass of juice for me, little pieces of toast with pâté, and a small birthday cake with one candle in the middle. After he put the tray down he snipped off one of the roses and put it in her hair.

He poured their drinks and proposed a toast to Miss Jones. Then we all clinked glasses and drank, and they kissed each other. Miss Jones was fingering a string of beautiful amber beads she hadn't worn before. "Jason's birthday present," she said. "Aren't they lovely?"

He must have given them to her in the kitchen. "Yeah," I said. I took my little box out of my pocket and gave it to her. "Happy birthday."

I think she liked it, although it didn't look like much next to the necklace. She kept going to the mirror to admire the beads while sipping her drink. I felt uncomfortable with them. They ate only a little bit of pâté and although I was starving, I didn't want to eat more than they did.

"We don't have too much time," Jason said. He was pacing around the room as if he were in a hurry.

"We have to have some cake with Annie," Miss Jones said.

mind me. I'm going to have to call
ler and wait for her to pick me up. You
ad."

e'll have some cake first," Miss Jones
said firmly. She cut the cake and gave us each a
slice.

"Cake and martinis, some combination," Jason said. He had sat down on the sofa, and
then rested his feet with his heavy boots
against a fragile table. I thought she was going
to scold him but she simply gave him a look
and didn't say anything. I was furious. There
was something about the way he sat there,
stuffing cake into his mouth, drinking his cock-
tail, that made me angry. He was so uncouth.

They had to leave but Miss Jones told me to
take my time, to call my mother and to wait for
her in the apartment as it was cold outside. She
said I could just close the outside door and it
would lock by itself.

Jason had been in such a hurry to leave that
they hadn't finished their drinks. The pitcher
still had some martinis in it, and the tray with
the food was on the round table where they'd
left it. I was hungry so I ate more pâté. It made
me thirsty so I finished Miss Jones's martini. It
tasted odd, a little like medicine, but it was
cold, and after it went down I felt warm. I sat

down on the sofa and looked around the room. It was so pretty. Our house always looked cluttered after I returned from here. This room seemed just like the old Miss Jones, ascetic, someone who went after "the essentials." "People decorate themselves, their homes, and their ideas with flimsy bits of nothing," she had said. I was never quite sure exactly what she meant, but I think I got the gist of it.

I got up and walked into the bedroom. It was a mess. They hadn't even made the bed. You could see the imprint of their heads on the pillows. Clothes were piled on the floor and on the chairs. Beautiful, fastidious Miss Jones! What an ass I was.

I went back to the living room and ate the rest of the pâté. (When I get nervous or angry I eat a lot.) Then I drank the rest of the martinis. Serves them right, I thought. If they hadn't wanted me to eat and drink their stuff they shouldn't have left it there. I sat there for a bit really feeling terrific, as if polishing off the food and drinking their martinis made me belong.

9

I don't know how long I sat there, but when I stood up I felt strange. I felt I had grown taller and that I could do anything—yet when I walked I had to be careful not to bump into furniture. It was very peculiar. When I got to the telephone I had to think for a few minutes to remember my number.

When I got Mom on the phone she kept asking, "Are you all right? Are you sure? You sound funny. . . ." We arranged to meet at a department store not far away. I felt sleepy when I hung up the phone so I washed my face with cold water, but I still felt odd.

Out on the street I felt worse than I had in

the house. There were too many cars and too many houses, and too much sun. I felt confused. I wasn't even sure I was walking in the right direction.

When I met Mom she took one look at me and said, "There *is* something the matter with you. I knew it on the phone. Your eyes are glazed and . . ." She pulled me close to her and said, "Annie, what on earth have you been drinking? You smell of gin. For God's sake, what did they give you?"

"We had some drinks and some pâté. It wasn't much of a party."

"Some drinks? *What* kind of drinks? Annie Kruger, you tell me exactly what you drank."

"They had a pitcher of martinis," I mumbled.

Mom looked furious. "And they gave you some?"

"I had a taste."

"You have had more than a taste. You smell like a bar. How much did you have? Tell me the truth."

"I don't know. Maybe two or three glasses. Not big tall glasses . . ."

"You had two or three martinis!" Mom shrieked so loud that people turned and stared.

"Shh-shh, Mom, don't shout." Her voice

hurt my ears. "I think I'm going to be sick."

"I shouldn't wonder," she said crisply. She grabbed me by the hand and led me to the escalator. "We'll be in the ladies' room in a minute. Try to control yourself."

We made it just in time. When I came out of the stall Mom washed my face with a wet paper towel and made me sit down. "That woman is crazy. Imagine giving a child martinis. A teacher, no less. It's hard to believe. . . . Is this her idea of being modern?"

"It wasn't her fault," I said, but Mom wasn't listening; she went on along the lines of what can you expect of a teacher who is living with a man and wears crazy clothes to school. I should have explained everything, but I felt as though I was going to be sick again. My head was getting fuzzier by the minute. "Mom, I've got to get out of here. Take me home, please." I felt as if the walls were closing in, and I knew the women in the ladies' room were staring.

"That woman shouldn't be teaching school," Mom said.

"Stop it!" I shouted. "Please forget it and take me home."

I got up and held on to Mom. "I have no intention of forgetting it," she said.

At home I went right up to my room, and

went to bed. I fell asleep right away. When I woke up I could hear voices downstairs. Mom hadn't said anything about having company that night; in fact, I remembered her saying that morning that she and Dad were going to have a quiet evening at home. She must have changed her mind. My head hurt, so I went to Mom's bathroom and took some aspirin. It was after eight o'clock, so I must have missed supper, but I wasn't hungry. I was about to go back to bed when my dad called me.

"Hey, Annie, you up? Come on down."

I didn't feel like moving, but I wanted to say hello to Dad since I hadn't seen him for a week.

When I stepped into the living room everyone stopped talking. Mom's best friend, Mimi Bernstein, and her husband were there, and the O'Connors, another couple my parents saw regularly. They were all staring at me. I kissed Dad, and Mrs. Bernstein said, "Are you all right, Annie? I hear you've had quite a day."

I gave Mom a dirty look. "I had to tell them, Annie," Mom said. "I don't think you understand that what Miss Jones did is very serious."

"No, I don't. It's no big deal." The whole thing was getting out of hand. They looked as if they were ready to hang Miss Jones, and I stared at them completely immobilized. I know I should have told them what had really happened but I didn't open my mouth. I tried to convince myself that it was Miss Jones's fault. I saw Jason's face dancing in front of me, and I thought of their bedroom. Let them believe what they want, I decided. It's not going to make any difference. In a day or two they'll forget all about it.

They started to question me. "Tell us just what happened." Mr. O'Connor puffed on his pipe and stared at me.

"Nothing happened. Miss Jones and her boyfriend were celebrating her birthday, and after my lesson we had a party. I don't know what you are all excited about."

Mr. O'Connor looked at my mother. "Is it true that she is living with a young man?"

My mother shrugged. "I don't know if he actually lives there, but he spends a lot of time there. Her landlady said that he sleeps there. Isn't that so, Annie?"

"How should I know? May I be excused now?"

"You are very fond of Miss Jones, aren't you, Annie?" asked Mrs. Bernstein. I suppose she meant to be sympathetic—she's a neat lady and I like her—but it was the wrong question at the wrong time. Did I like Miss Jones? I had loved her and now I hated her. I could feel the tears welling up and I ran out of the room. I wished I had a lock on my bedroom door but I didn't think my mother would come upstairs when all those people were downstairs.

I cried the way I don't remember ever having cried before. I wished that I had someone to talk to, but there was no one. I knew I was in a mess. I also knew that if I told the truth, I would be in another mess. I would have to face them all and say I'd lied. It wouldn't have been easy, but it would have been better. But I couldn't do it. Call me stupid; call me rotten. I just didn't have the courage. I don't know if anything could have made me go downstairs and tell those people the truth.

I convinced myself that it would all blow over; by tomorrow they'd be talking about something else, and by Monday they'd have forgotten it entirely.

I hadn't counted on Mr. McDermott. I didn't even know Mr. McDermott. But he was a friend of the O'Connors, and he was on the school board. They told him about it, and he became furious. It was the kind of thing he enjoyed. He loved to fight against things like sex education in the schools, and he thought we should say prayers in school. You can imagine what he thought of Miss Jones living with a man she wasn't married to—and giving martinis to a kid.

But I didn't find out about Mr. McDermott until Monday. On Sunday I stayed in bed. Mom and Dad went out, so there wasn't a chance to talk. I liked having the house to myself. I slept most of the afternoon, watched some TV at night, and was asleep before my parents came home.

I stayed in bed late Monday morning so there wouldn't be time to talk to Mom. I drank a glass of milk and ran for my bus. Nothing happened the first two periods and I was beginning to think that nothing was going to happen, when I was called into the principal's office.

I was shaking as I walked down the hall. Mr. Keane wasn't alone. Mrs. O'Connor was there, and I was introduced to Mr. McDermott. Mr. Keane smiled, and Mrs. O'Connor looked nervous. I knew right away I wasn't going to like Mr. McDermott. He had one of those smiles that's worse than nothing.

Mr. Keane pointed to a chair and said, "Sit down. No reason for you to be nervous, Annie.

We would just like to ask you a few questions. Why don't we start by your telling us exactly what happened at Miss Jones's on Saturday."

"There's nothing much to tell. It was her birthday and after my lesson we had a party. It wasn't anything special."

"She served liquor, didn't she?" Mr. McDermott looked at me sternly.

"They had some drinks," I said. I turned to Mrs. O'Connor. "It wasn't anything much, honest."

"You've been quite friendly with Miss Jones, haven't you?" Mr. Keane was tapping his fingers on his desk. I wished he'd stop.

"Yes, I guess so."

"Did she ever give you anything to drink before?"

"No, sir, never."

"Did she ever offer you anything else? A cigarette or marijuana?" Mr. McDermott leaned toward me eagerly.

"No, of course not. Never. She'd never do anything like that."

"But she served you martinis," he said triumphantly.

"That wasn't so terrible," I murmured.

"Are you accustomed to drinking liquor?" he demanded.

"No, sir, but we were celebrating her birthday."

"I think that's enough," Mr. Keane said soothingly. "It is a serious offense for a teacher to serve alcohol to a youngster. We're all very sorry that it happened."

"But it wasn't in school. It was in her house. That has nothing to do with school."

"She is a teacher in our school and you are a pupil," Mr. Keane said sternly.

"May I be excused now?" I got up to leave.

Mr. Keane looked at Mr. McDermott and Mrs. O'Connor. "Any more questions?" he asked.

Mr. McDermott fixed his pale eyes on me. "Yes. I want to know if a man is living with Miss Jones?"

"How should I know?" I said.

"You go to her house regularly for your music lesson, don't you? Surely you would know if someone was living with her? We expect you to tell the truth."

"I don't know," I said. "I have my music lesson and leave. I don't know anything about her private life."

"That is hard to believe," Mr. McDermott said flatly.

"You can go now," Mr. Keane said more kindly. "I'd rather you didn't talk about this to anyone, Annie. Let's just keep it to ourselves for the time being."

"Yes, sir." I certainly wasn't going to talk about it. I wished everyone would forget about it.

10

When I came out of school that Monday, Miss Jones was waiting for me. "I'd like to talk to you, Annie," she said. "Have you got a few minutes?"

"I've got to get my bus," I told her.

"I have my car; I'll drive you home. Perhaps we can have a cup of tea someplace where we can talk."

"Okay." I didn't want to talk to her, but I knew I had to. My stomach was in knots.

We got into her car and drove to a shopping center that had a coffee shop. Neither of us spoke much. When we were settled at a table and she had ordered tea and toasted muffins for both of us, she said, "I suppose you know that Mr. Keane called me into his office, and I'm sure you know what he wanted to talk about." She put her elbows on the table and leaned across to me. "Why did you do it, Annie? Why did you make up such a story?"

I looked away. I thought about pretending I didn't know what she was talking about, but I decided that would be stupid. I looked up at her again. "I don't know. It just happened. I didn't think it would matter. I don't know why everyone's so excited."

She studied my face for a few minutes. "I don't believe it 'just happened.' Stories like that don't just happen; they come out of somewhere. You wanted to hurt me, didn't you?"

"No, I didn't. Honestly. I didn't think about it, that's all. I wasn't thinking about anything."

"But you must have finished those martinis for a reason. You could have telephoned your mother right away and sat quietly until she arrived. I think you were angry, Annie. Very angry. You've been angry and probably hurt ever since I've been going with Jason. Think about it."

"Well, I did think it was kind of funny after

all the things you said for you to all of a sudden have a boyfriend. And to have him live with you . . ."

"Do you find that shocking? I mean for us to live together and not be married?"

"I don't care about whether you're married or not." I spilled a little tea on my blouse and wiped it off with a napkin.

"What *do* you care about? What's bothering you?" She poured more tea for both of us.

I didn't want to answer. I couldn't tell her the truth and I couldn't think of anything else to say.

"Try to tell me," she coaxed. "It's important. Don't be afraid."

"I guess I was jealous of Jason. I mean, you were alone, and I was alone, and then you weren't alone anymore. That's part of it." My voice was low, and she was leaning over so that she could hear me. "I guess I felt you weren't my friend anymore, and that you had changed." I looked up and met her eyes. "I thought you were special."

"But I'm really not different. I'm the same Annabel Jones that I was before. I feel the same about you, that we are friends. I feel the same about my music, and my thoughts and ideas haven't changed. Falling in love with Jason has broadened me—it has made my world bigger, that's all. When you're older and fall in love, you'll know what I mean." Her face was flushed and she looked very pretty.

"You and my mother keep telling me that. I'm not going to fall in love. And I'm tired of hearing about me and boys."

"You sound pretty vehement. Have you had a bad experience with a boy? That boy, Brian, the one you were down in the gorge with—he seems like a nice boy. Did he give you a hard time?"

"No, Brian didn't do anything. . . . No boy's ever given me a hard time. It's not that, it's . . .." I could feel the tears well up in my eyes and I was afraid I was going to start crying.

Miss Jones reached out and took my hand. I blew my nose into the paper napkin, but I couldn't keep the tears back. I felt ridiculous crying, but we were in a booth and no one could see me. "I don't think I can talk about it."

"I think you should. Maybe I can help you."

"Not anymore. I thought you could, before you started going with Jason, but not now. I wanted to be different, like you. . . . I mean, not care about having a boyfriend and all that stuff."

Miss Jones interrupted me. "But I always cared about having a boyfriend. Many a night I cried myself to sleep because I was lonely. You don't understand. . . . All the things you and I have talked about—wanting to have a life that didn't value material things so much—none of that excluded having a companion. I want to share my life with someone, and I am very happy that Jason and I found each other. We think the same way about so many things."

"You and Jason?"

"Don't look so surprised. Of course we do; otherwise we wouldn't love each other so much. I'll tell you a secret. I haven't told anyone yet, but we plan to get married in the summer." She was beaming.

I guess I still looked surprised because she laughed and said, "I'm sorry you don't like him."

"It's not that. . . ." I was thinking of her bedroom and how strange it had been to see his things strewn all over it.

"Sometimes we stay up all night talking. I don't think we'll ever run out of things to talk about."

"I can never think of anything to say to a boy."

She laughed again. "That's because you think a boy is some strange animal. It's your age. I remember very well how I felt. You want to be with boys yet you're afraid of them. Afraid they won't like you, afraid that they're going to kiss you, and afraid because you want them to. You're at a difficult yet wonderful age, Annie; don't be afraid. Don't be afraid of your feelings. You're a lovely person, in spite of what you did, and all the feelings you're having—about boys, about yourself—are healthy and normal. You'll work them out." She looked at her watch. "I think we have to go now. I hope you will tell Mr. Keane the truth tomorrow morning." She picked up the check and looked at me questioningly.

"I'll try. Why don't you tell him? Tell him that I lied."

She shook her head. "I have already told him that your story wasn't true but it has to come from you. And no one can do it for you."

"I'll think about it," was all I could say.

Miss Jones dropped me off at my house but I didn't go inside. I had too much to think about and I didn't feel like talking to my mother. I knew she was home because her car was in the driveway. It was still light out so I went to the park and scrambled up the hill onto the path. It was very peaceful. I was thinking more about what Miss Jones had said than about talking to Mr. Keane. She had said I was lovely and that my feelings were healthy and normal—but how did she know? Yet from the way she had spoken I had the feeling that when she was my age she had felt the same way, and that made me feel better.

I walked until I got to the path that led to the gorge, but I sat down at the top. I didn't feel like going down. It was warm in the sun but every time a cloud passed I shivered. I didn't care. I wouldn't have minded getting sick and staying in bed for a few days. For the hundredth time I went over the whole thing again, from the time Miss Jones left with Jason until I met my mother. If I had only spoken up then . . .

I was still sitting there when Brian came up from the gorge. He took me by surprise. "What are you doing here?" I squinted up at him, against the sun. His cheeks were pink as usual.

"The same as you. Just sitting and thinking."

"I didn't think boys did that. I mean . . ." I was embarrassed and I didn't finish.

"You sure have some crazy ideas. People are people."

"I know that."

He kept looking at me and then he sat down. "I hear you got Miss Jones into a lot of trouble. She may get fired. It's too bad; she's the nicest teacher we have."

"Who told you?"

"My mom. I guess everybody knows. Mr. McDermott's been calling people. Mom says he's on the warpath."

"I wish he'd fall in the lake. He's making a big thing out of nothing."

Brian looked at me curiously. "But she did give you some martinis, didn't she? That was pretty dumb."

"Maybe."

"Maybe what?"

"I'm sick of talking about it."

"I thought you liked Miss Jones." Brian had picked up a stick and was making circles in the dirt.

"I do like her. What's that got to do with it?"

"You didn't have to tell anybody."

"I didn't tell. My mother guessed, and besides . . ."

"Besides what?"

"Stop asking me questions," I yelled. He looked hurt and I felt awful. I started crying. "Damn it!" I blubbered.

Brian didn't know what to do. He stood up; then he sat down. After a while he put his hand on my shoulder, and gave me his red bandana handkerchief. He looked so upset that I started to giggle. "I knew you didn't wear stuff on your eyes," Brian said.

I blew my nose and wiped my face. "Who said I did?"

"Some of the kids. They said your eyelashes weren't real. If you used that stuff it would be running now, wouldn't it? My mom's runs when her eyes tear."

"I don't wear that stuff," I said indignantly. "Brian, I'm in trouble."

"About Miss Jones?"

"Yeah. I did something awful. It's hard to talk about it."

"Don't talk about it if you don't want to." He sat on a rock next to me.

"I've got to. Promise you won't tell anyone?"

"Cross my heart and hope to die," he said solemnly.

"She didn't do it. Miss Jones didn't give me anything to drink. I drank the martinis after she and her boyfriend had left." I was terrified. He'd probably never want to talk to me again.

"You mean you made it up?" I thought he was going to start laughing.

"It's not funny. I didn't exactly make it up. It just happened. I didn't do it deliberately. It's very complicated."

I told him the whole story. He kept shaking his head as if he couldn't believe what I was telling him. "You mean you stayed there by yourself and finished off their booze? Didn't you get sick?"

"I did. That was the trouble. That's how my mother knew I'd been drinking. It was awful."

Now he did laugh. "You're crazy, Annie." But the way he said it made me feel like he liked me even if I was weird.

"Miss Jones wants me to tell Mr. Keane the truth. I know I should, but I can't face everyone and say I made up a story like that. It sounds so awful and stupid now, but when it happened, when I let my mother think it was Miss Jones's fault, it seemed unimportant."

I wanted him to agree with me but he looked at me as if he weren't quite sure. "You must have known that what you had done was wrong," he said. "I mean drinking the stuff. Then I guess you wanted to blame her instead of yourself."

"You make it sound awful. That's not very nice."

"But it's true, isn't it?"

"You're being mean. I'm sorry I talked to you." I got up and began to walk away, but Brian stopped me.

"Don't get mad. But there's no point saying you're sorry and telling them the truth, if you don't know what you're sorry about. You'll always feel that everyone's been unfair. I'm just trying to sort things out."

"Yeah. To make me look like a jerk."

"Will you just listen to me? I don't think you deliberately wanted to get Miss Jones into trouble—maybe you did and maybe you didn't, but that's not so important. Tell them the truth. You were ashamed to say that you sat there and drank the stuff by yourself, so you let your mother think Miss Jones had given it to you. You didn't know it was going to hurt her. That doesn't make you sound like a jerk."

"I'll try," I said.

We walked back to my house, together, Brian holding my hand. I felt that I wasn't all alone anymore. It was funny to think of Brian as a friend—not just as a boy, worrying about kissing and that stuff, but as a person. But still I was glad that before we came out of the woods he stopped and kissed me.

11

 When I got home that afternoon
Mom was frantic. "Where have you been? I've
been calling all over to find you. You weren't
on the bus."

"I know. I stopped to have tea with Miss
Jones."

"Miss Jones?" Mom shrieked. "What on
earth did you do that for?"

"She asked me. She wanted to talk to me."

Mom stood with her arms folded across her
chest and faced me angrily. "I daresay she did.
Annie, I don't want you to have anything more
to do with her. She's done enough harm already. I hope they fire her. Mr. McDermott has

invited a few parents and some board members to his house tonight to discuss this whole thing. He wants you to come."

"What for? He doesn't need me. I'm not going." I was scared. I didn't want to face a bunch of people that night. I needed time to think, to decide what I was going to do. I knew what I had to do, but to do it was something else. I had to get up my courage; I needed time.

"You certainly are going. Don't you give me a hard time, Annie Kruger. If you had any sense you wouldn't have drunk that stuff even when she gave it to you. You should have known better."

I didn't answer. What was she going to say when she found out that I'd done it on my own? My heart dropped. Would I ever be able to face her, to face the others, especially that horrid Mr. McDermott, and tell them the truth?

Mr. McDermott's house was just like him and his homely wife: overly neat and colorless. It was the kind of house where you're afraid to sit down for fear of rumpling a cushion, except most of the chairs were hard and had no cushions.

I didn't know most of the people there. Mrs. Bernstein's was the only friendly face. The others tried to be friendly—you know: "That poor child, what a terrible thing to do to her . . ." Blah, blah, blah. But I had a funny feeling some of them were thinking it was my fault, that I must have done something to make them think I'd drink with them. Wait until they heard the truth.

Mr. McDermott introduced me and told me to sit down. Then he began to talk in his pompous way. "We have a very serious problem here, ladies and gentlemen, and I asked you here this evening so we could informally discuss the best way to handle it. You all know what happened to this child, and I asked her to be here so that later if you wish to ask any questions, you may. I believe that the first order of business would be for all of us to agree, and I trust that we will, that Miss Jones should be fired. Whether to permit her to finish out the school year is the main question." He held his fingers in a tent formation in front of him and looked around the room, peering over his glasses.

"I think that's rushing it a bit," one man said quietly. He looked younger than the others. "First let's discuss just how serious this is."

"I think it's very serious. My daughter was given hard liquor by a woman who teaches in our school and invites children to go out with her." I gave my mother a dirty look but she paid no attention.

"I agree," said another woman. "It's very serious indeed."

"But doesn't she have a contract?" one of the men asked. "Can we break a contract for something she did out of school?"

"The corruption of a minor is pertinent and serious whether it's in school or out of school," Mr. McDermott said tersely.

"Come on," the young man said. "You make it sound as if the child were assaulted and raped. It was a stupid thing for Miss Jones to do, but it wasn't criminal."

They argued back and forth, back and forth. I kept thinking, Annie, speak up, tell them the truth. But my tongue felt glued in my mouth. It was crazy, and I kept feeling worse and worse. Every time I thought I could do it, I looked around the room and saw all those faces and felt sick to my stomach.

I was concentrating hard on not getting sick and wishing I could run away, when I heard Mr. McDermott say, "I intend to recommend to the school board that we let her go immediately. She is not a fit person to be in our school system."

I sat up and without thinking at all, I yelled, "That's not true. She's a wonderful teacher."

Everyone looked at me. "She is a good music teacher," my mother said quietly. "We can't take that away from her."

"She's a good person," I said, looking straight at my mother. "I'm the one who's no good. I made it up. She never gave me the liquor. I drank it after they left."

I sat back in my chair. My mother came over to me and put her arm around me. "Are you all right? You look very white. . . ."

I turned my face and buried it against her, and cried. But I could still hear Mr. McDermott. "Obviously the child is upset and who can blame her? But equally obvious is the fact that she is trying to protect her teacher. We mustn't let that influence us."

"I'm not protecting her," I yelled. "I'm telling you the truth. I drank the martinis when they left. Miss Jones gave me fruit juice." I looked around the room at the others. "You've got to believe me."

My mother knelt down by my chair and cupped my face in her hands. "Are you telling the truth, Annie?"

"Yes, honestly, Mom, I swear I am."

She stood up and sighed. "I believe her." She pulled a chair over next to mine and sat down.

Everyone started to talk at once. After a while the younger man took over. "I think this meeting can come to an end." He turned to me. "You should be the one to tell Miss Jones and to apologize to her. The principal should too. I think we should all go home."

There was more buzzing, and people got up to leave. A few came over and patted me on the shoulder. Mrs. Bernstein was one of them. "I'm glad you spoke up," she said. "You'll be glad you did."

Mr. McDermott was as mean as ever. "I hope you're telling the truth now," he said. "If you were my child you'd get a good whipping for telling such a horrible lie." You can bet I was glad I wasn't his child.

Mom was very quiet on the way home. When we were in the kitchen she said, "Do you want to talk about it now, or wait until the morning?"

"I'd just as soon get it over with now," I said.

She put on the kettle for tea and sat down at the kitchen table. She looked very tired. "Why don't you tell me what did happen. The true story this time."

After I had finished she said, "Why did you let me think that Miss Jones had given you the liquor?"

"It was easier. I wasn't thinking, and it just happened. I was ashamed to tell you."

Mom stood up to fix the tea. "I don't think you're telling me all of it. I think there's more to it than that. Were you angry with Miss Jones?"

"A little."

"What do you mean by that?" Mom turned to me impatiently. "For heaven's sake, Annie, you've caused enough trouble. Tell me everything." She poured us each a cup of tea and sat down again. I got some cookies, and started to eat them nervously. I looked at Mom and then down at my teacup.

"I was jealous of Miss Jones. It sounds stupid when I say it—but I was jealous of her having a boyfriend and acting like other people. I had thought she was special."

Mom looked at me in amazement. "You can be special and still have a boyfriend. Oh, Annie . . ." She leaned over and put her arms around me, but there were tears in her eyes.

"You've been alone too much. Was it because you didn't feel you could talk to me?"

"I don't think so. It was different. When Caroline started going with Ken, Miss Jones became my only friend. And when she started going with Jason, I wanted to hurt her." I was feeling sick from all the cookies I'd been stuffing in my mouth.

"You have hurt her, I hope not too badly. But what about you? You're going to have to be punished. I don't think you should go scot-free, do you?"

"Whatever you say. I just want to get it all over with. Miss Jones already knows it's not true; do I have to talk to her again?"

"You certainly do. You have to apologize to her."

"Okay. Can I go to bed now?"

Mom gave me a long look before she kissed me goodnight. "Get a good sleep."

Looking back now it seems as if it all happened a million years ago. Yet there are some things about the next day that are so sharp I will never forget them. The color of my room when I woke up: Everything was a purplish gray. There was a heavy mist outside and dark clouds moving my way. I banged my window closed and turned on the light, which made it worse. I turned the light off and dressed in a room that was neither dark nor light. I had been sick during the night but I didn't tell Mom. I felt that nothing would ever be the same again, that I had lost something I would never be able to replace. How could I when I didn't know what I had lost?

It was a great relief to have told Mom the truth. I didn't care too much about the other people, but I wanted to see Miss Jones and get that over with. I wasn't looking forward to talking to Mr. Keane but I felt that the worst was behind me. Mrs. Bernstein had said I'd be glad, and I was.

I went downstairs to practice my piano sonata for about half an hour before I had to leave for school. I had been practicing almost every morning, but that morning I couldn't concentrate. I kept making mistakes so I stopped playing and just sat at the piano. I felt I was at a turning point in my life. Mom always said I dramatized things too much, but I wasn't making anything up that day: I had lost Miss Jones. It was almost worse than someone dying. On the surface it would be the same but the closeness would be gone. I didn't have a single close friend. Brian had been nice, but I was sure he had felt sorry for me, and that's not the same as being a close friend.

I hadn't minded before because I had talked myself into thinking that being a loner was romantic, but now it seemed sad.

"You don't look well," Mom said to me at breakfast.

"I'm okay. What's my punishment going to be?"

"I don't know. I'll discuss it with your father when he comes home." She looked at me as if she wanted to say more, but she didn't. Mom and I were never going to be close. I mean, we got along okay but I never felt really close to her.

The minute I got to school I went to Miss Jones's room. She wasn't there so I watered her plants and gave them some plant food. They looked a little droopy. I was still busy with them when she came in.

"Thanks, Annie. They needed some attention," she said.

"I told them last night," I said quickly.

"You told what to whom?"

"Mr. McDermott had a bunch of parents at his house. I told them the truth. I'm very sorry for what I did. I'm sorry for what happened."

"I'm sure you are. Thank you, Annie."

We just stood looking at each other. "I suppose you're mad at me," I said.

"I was angry, very angry. This could have cost me my job. I was hurt, too. I didn't understand how you could do such a thing. I think you live too much in your own world. You know, the real world's often better than what you make up."

"You think so? I don't."

She smiled. "You're awfully stubborn. Give the world a chance, Annie; don't run away from it."

"Yes, Miss Jones."

She looked at me and shrugged as if to say, "I give up." But instead she said, "I let you down—at least you thought so—and you struck back. We should be even now, shouldn't we? Can we go back and start from square one?"

"I guess so." But I knew we couldn't, and I knew she knew we couldn't.

"Do you want me to go with you to see Mr. Keane? Or would you rather go alone?"

"I don't mind if you come with me."

She patted my arm. "Annie, it's not the end of the world. You made a bad mistake, but you owned up to it, and that's a big step forward. People are more forgiving than you think they are."

Together we went to Mr. Keane's office.

I must say he was decent. He listened to me without saying anything. He just looked at me intently, and then he asked the same question Mom had: "Are you telling the truth now?"

"Yes, sir, I am." I looked to Miss Jones for confirmation.

"I'm afraid she is. I'm not condoning what she did, but I think I understand why she did it. I don't think it's necessary to go into more detail. It's really irrelevant."

I gave her a grateful look.

"You could have gotten Miss Jones into a lot of trouble," Mr. Keane said. "I'm sure she's had some sleepless nights over this incident." Mr. Keane turned to Miss Jones. "What do you think her punishment should be?"

"I've been thinking about it. Perhaps she could be dropped from the music festival. She was going to play a solo."

"Oh, I've worked so hard on it! Couldn't it be something else?" I looked from one to the other.

They exchanged glances and Mr. Keane

said, "No. Playing in a concert is a privilege and you don't deserve any privileges now. You're getting off easy."

"My parents are going to punish me too."

"I hope you've learned your lesson, Annie—especially about deliberately hurting someone else. It was a very selfish thing to do."

"I know it. I'm very sorry."

When we left Mr. Keane's office, Miss Jones said, "I'm sorry things worked out this way. I . expected you to be the star of the concert."

I had nothing to say. I was heartbroken. When I left school at three o'clock it didn't make me feel any better to see Miss Jones go off cheerfully with Jason. I turned away; I didn't feel like watching them. I wasn't jealous anymore, just depressed. As I started walking home, Brian fell into step with me.

"Want to go for a soda?" he asked.

"Okay."

"I know you're used to drinking martinis, but I haven't got my ID card with me." He grinned.

"Stop it," I said. It felt good when he held my hand. When we were drinking our sodas, he said, "Want to go to the movies next Saturday? Not just with me, with Caroline and Ken, and Sheila and whoever she's going with this week."

"That would be neat."

"Okay, it's a date—don't forget."

I felt better by the time I got home. My father was there and before we ate I told him what had happened. He was angry. "What you did was senseless and mean."

"I know. You don't have to rub it in." I should have waited until after he ate.

We didn't talk much while we were eating. I told Mom about my date with Brian.

"I don't think she should go," Dad said. "She should stay home."

"Dad, you can't do that. It's my first date, the first time a boy has asked me out. I have to go."

"You don't have to do anything," he said. He turned to my mother. "Don't you think that should be her punishment?"

Mom hesitated. "It might be a little harsh. She did tell the truth."

"I don't care. Staying home one night isn't the end of the world."

"He'll never ask me out again!"

"Don't be dramatic," Dad said. "You have a lifetime ahead of you."

"You don't understand."

"That's what you always say." My father lit a cigar.

"That's because it's true."

"I don't understand why you did what you did, that's for sure."

I turned to my mother. "Please make him change his mind."

She looked at my father but he was adamant.

The next day in school when everyone was practicing for the concert, I read some books about music that Miss Jones had given me. They were boring.

After school I waited for Brian. He seemed glad to see me and we started walking toward the village. "I haven't any money for a soda today," Brian said.

"That's okay. I haven't either or I'd treat. But I have to tell you something. I can't go out with you Saturday night."

He looked hurt. "Something better came along?"

"No, nothing like that. It's my punishment, for you know what."

His face lit up. "Do you feel bad about it?"

"I feel awful."

"I'm glad." He took my hand. "It must mean that you like me."

"You don't have to look so pleased about my having to stay home."

"You didn't hear what I said."

"Yes, I did. You said I must like you."

"So? You're supposed to answer that." He glanced at me quickly. Then he turned and stared at me.

"I do like you," I said.

He squeezed my hand. "That's good because I like you too. Don't worry, we'll go out the next Saturday night."

We walked hand in hand. Not being good in math, I tried, but couldn't figure out in my head how many hours it was going to be until a week from Saturday night.

About the Author

HILA COLMAN was born and raised in New York City and attended Radcliffe College. She began writing books for young people after writing stories and articles for magazines. Ms. Colman writes nearly every day and her mind is always a few ideas ahead of her typewriter. She is the author of numerous award-winning books stemming from an interest in the problems of adolescence. Her books often explore family relationships, which she feels directly affect young people's attitudes and lives.

Archway paperbacks by Hila Colman include *Accident; Claudia, Where Are You?; Confession of a Storyteller; Diary of a Frantic Kid Sister; Don't Tell Me That You Love Me; Nobody Has to Be a Kid Forever; Tell Me No Lies;* and *What's the Matter with the Dobsons?*

Besides writing, Hila Colman enjoys traveling and is active in politics, serving on several town committees and as a trustee of her local library. She lives in Bridgewater, Connecticut, and has two sons, both of whom are married.